The Pentagon

Ted and Lola Schaefer

Heinemann Library
Chicago, Illinois

Designed by Richard Parker and Mike Hogg Design
Illustrations by Jeff Edwards
Originated by Chroma Graphics (Overseas) Pte Ltd.
Printed and bound in China by South China Printing Company

10 09 08 07
10 9 8 7 6 5 4 3 2

Library of Congress Cataloging-in-Publication Data
Schaefer, Ted, 1948-
  The Pentagon / Ted and Lola M. Schaefer.
     p. cm. -- (Symbols of freedom)
  Includes index.
  ISBN 1-4034-6663-7 (library binding-hardcover) -- ISBN 1-4034-6672-6 (pbk.)
  ISBN 978-1-4034-6663-1 (library binding-hardcover) -- ISBN 978-1-4034-6672-3 (pbk.)
  1. Pentagon (Va.)--Juvenile literature. I. Schaefer, Lola M., 1950- II. Title. III. Series.
  UA26.A727S33 2005
  355.6'0973--dc22
                          2005002040

Acknowledgments
The publishers would like to thank the following for permission to reproduce photographs:
Corbis p. 19 (Annie Griffiths Belt), 8 (Bettman), 16, 22 (Reuters), 7, 25 (Sygma), 21 (Sygma/Jacques Langevin); Department of Defence pp. 27 (Chief Petty Officer Johnny Bivera, U.S. Navy), 17 (Petty Officer 2nd Class Elizabeth A. Edwards, U.S. Navy), 4 (Tech. Sgt. Andy Dunaway, U.S. Air Force), 26 (R. D. Ward); Getty Images pp. 15 (AFP), 10 (Hulton Archive), 9, 20, 23 (Time & Life Pictures); Jill Birschbach/Harcourt Education Ltd pp. 5, 6, 12, 13, 14, 18, 24, 28, 29; Library of Congress p. 11 (Theodor Horydczak Collection).

Cover photograph of the Pentagon reproduced with permission of Getty Images/Taxi.

The publishers would like to thank Brett Easton and William Hopper for their assistance in the preparation of this book.

Every effort has been made to contact copyright holders of any material reproduced in this book. Any omissions will be rectified in subsequent printings if notice is given to the publishers.

The publishers and authors have done their best to ensure the accuracy and currency of all the information in this book, however, they can accept no responsibility for any loss, injury, or inconvenience sustained as a result of information or advice contained in the book.

Some words are shown in bold, **like this**. You can find out what they mean by looking in the glossary.

Contents

The Pentagon

The Pentagon is a huge, five-sided building with walls of stone. It is in Arlington, Virginia, across the Potomac River from Washington, D.C.

The Pentagon is the home of the
Department of Defense. People there work
to keep the **military** strong. They keep the
United States safe and protect its **freedom**.

The Department of Defense

The **Department of Defense** is in charge of all the **military** forces. These forces are the Army, Navy, Marine Corps, Air Force, and the Coast Guard.

The U.S. **military** serves in many countries around the world. The Department of Defense must keep these **troops supplied** and tell them what to do.

Building the Pentagon

In 1941 the **Department of Defense** had seventeen office buildings in Washington, D.C. They were all too crowded. The Department of Defense needed more room.

The government planned a new building for the Department of Defense. Building began on September 11, 1941. They thought it would take eight years to build.

World War II

On December 7, 1941, the United States **base** at Pearl Harbor was **attacked**. The country was now at war. Many new people joined the **military** and **Department of Defense**.

Work on the Pentagon moved more quickly. Thirteen thousand people worked day and night. An eight-year job was finished in less than two years.

A City in a Building

The Pentagon is one of the biggest office buildings in the world. Just like a city, it has banks, barbershops, stores, restaurants, and libraries.

The building has a **courtyard** in the center. The Pentagon covers as much land as 34 football fields. It has 284 bathrooms, 7,754 windows, and miles of hallways.

Working at the Pentagon

More than 26,000 people work in the Pentagon. Most of them are **military**, but many **civilians** work there, too. They all have important jobs.

The Pentagon never closes. Different people are there day and night. Work goes on seven days a week, every week of the year.

Mission of the Pentagon

Keeping the United States safe is the job of the U.S. **military**. Helping the military is the job of the Pentagon.

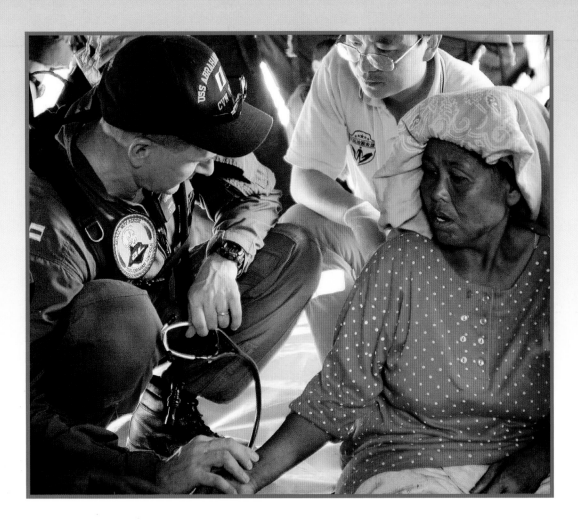

People in the **Department of Defense** send
military forces where they are needed. They
make sure the soldiers have the right
supplies to do their jobs.

In Times of Peace

The Pentagon must keep the **military** strong, even in times of peace. After war starts it is too late to get ready. Soldiers must always be **training**.

People at the Pentagon help soldiers learn the best ways to fight and protect themselves. Well-trained soldiers will not get hurt as much in a war.

In Times of War

When the country is at war, the **Department of Defense** watches the enemy. It finds out where they are and what they are doing.

People at the Pentagon are always talking with the U.S. military. They tell the soldiers about the enemy and the best ways to fight them.

Surprise Attack

On September 11, 2001, the Pentagon was **attacked** for the first time. **Terrorists** crashed an airplane into the west side of the building.

Terrorists hurt people and they can strike
without warning. This surprise attack
killed 184 people at the Pentagon site on
that sad day.

War on Terror

September 11, 2001

Today the Pentagon has been repaired. People there are working harder than ever. They are fighting a new kind of war. It is a war on **terrorism**.

In this war, information is very important.
The government tries to learn where
terrorists are hiding. Then the Pentagon
sends soldiers to fight them.

When You Visit the Pentagon

The only way you can visit the Pentagon is on a group tour. As you go through the halls, you will see many people busy at their jobs.

Civilians at the Pentagon work side by side with the U.S. **military**. Together, they keep the country safe and protect American freedom.

The Pentagon

★ The Pentagon has miles of hallways. The design includes walkways that lead from the center courtyard to the outside of the building, like spokes in a wheel.

★ On September 11, 1941, work began on the Pentagon. Exactly 60 years later, on September 11, 2001, **terrorists attacked** the Pentagon.

★ The courtyard in the center of the Pentagon covers about the size of five football fields. Pentagon workers relax in this outdoor area. They can eat lunch, talk with friends, or just enjoy a beautiful day.

★ The Pentagon has 16 parking lots that hold 8,770 cars. The government built miles of new highways to the Pentagon so people could get to work more quickly and easily.

Timeline

The Pentagon

* 1941   Work begins on the Pentagon

* 1941   Japanese attack **Pearl Harbor** and the United States enters **World War II**

* 1942   First office workers move into the Pentagon

* 1943   Pentagon is finished and **dedicated**

* 1949   War Department becomes **Department of Defense**

* 1976   The Pentagon Tour Program is set up

* 2001   September 11 – terrorists crash an airplane into the west side of the Pentagon

* 2002   September 11 – Pentagon workers move back into new and repaired offices

Glossary

attack try to hurt someone or something

base place from which an army, or another branch of the armed forces, is controlled

civilian someone who is not a member of the armed forces

courtyard open area with walls on all sides

dedicate have a ceremony that opens a new bridge, hospital, or memorial

Department of Defense part of the government that controls the military forces

freedom having the right to say, behave, or move about as you please

memorial something that is built to help people remember a person or an event

military having to do with soldiers, the armed forces, or war

Pearl Harbor name of the U.S. Naval base in the state of Hawaii

supplies food, materials, or tools needed

terrorism violent way of trying to make a government change something by using force against its civilians

terrorist someone who uses violence against civilians to try and get the government to change something

training learning and practicing the skills needed to do a particular job

troops soldiers

World War II war in which the United States, Great Britain, France, the Soviet Union, and other allied nations beat Germany, Italy, and Japan. The war began in 1939 and ended in 1945.

More Books to Read

An older reader can help you with these books.

Britton, Tamara. *The Pentagon*. Edina, Minn.: ABDO, 2003.

DeGezelle, Terri. *The Pentagon*. Mankato, Minn.: Capstone Press, 2004.

Lalley, Patrick. *September 11 2001: Terrorists Attack the U.S.* Chicago, Ill.: Heinemann Library, 2003.

Visiting the Pentagon

All guided tours of the Pentagon are free, Monday through Friday. Tours are not given on weekends or Federal holidays. Tours of the Pentagon are available to schools, educational organizations, and other select groups. Groups interested in touring the Pentagon should contact the Pentagon Tour Office.

Index

Schaefer, Ted, 1948-
The Pentagon /